Every Story Is a Call to Action

David A. Robertson

Every Story Is a Call to Action

CLC KREISEL LECTURE SERIES

UNIVERSITY *of* **ALBERTA** PRESS

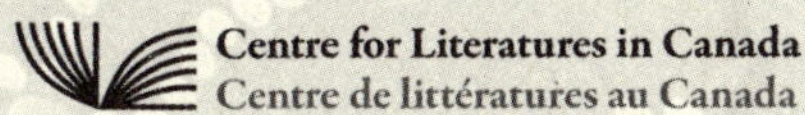

Centre for Literatures in Canada
Centre de littératures au Canada

Published by

University of Alberta Press
1-16 Rutherford Library South
11204 89 Avenue NW
Edmonton, Alberta, Canada T6G 2J4
amiskwaciwâskahikan | Treaty 6 | Métis
Territory
ualbertapress.ca | uapress@ualberta.ca
and
Centre for Literatures in Canada /
Centre de littératures au Canada
4-115 Humanities Centre
University of Alberta
Edmonton, Alberta, Canada T6G 2E5
www.uab.ca/clc

LIBRARY AND ARCHIVES CANADA
CATALOGUING IN PUBLICATION

Title: Every story is a call to action / David A.
    Robertson.
Names: Robertson, David, 1977– author
Series: Henry Kreisel lecture series.
Description: Series statement: CLC Kreisel
    lecture series | Includes bibliographical
    references.
Identifiers: Canadiana (print) 20250308681 |
    Canadiana (ebook) 20250323176 | ISBN
    9781772128512 (softcover) | ISBN
    9781772128581 (EPUB) |
    ISBN 9781772128598 (PDF)
Subjects: LCSH: Authorship—Social aspects.
    | LCSH: Authorship—Political aspects.
    | LCSH: Literature and society. | LCSH:
    Storytelling—Social aspects. | LCSH:
    Social justice in literature. | LCSH: Social
    change in literature. | LCSH: Rhetoric. |
    LCSH: Canada—Race relations. | LCSH:
    Canada—Ethnic relations. | LCSH:
    Reconciliation.
Classification: LCC PN149 .R63 2026 | DDC
    808.06/63—dc23

First edition, first printing, 2026.
First printed and bound in Canada by
Houghton Boston Printers, Saskatoon,
Saskatchewan.
Copyediting and proofreading by Joanne Muzak.

University of Alberta Press is committed to
protecting our natural environment. As part
of our efforts, this book is printed on Enviro
Paper: it contains 100% post-consumer
recycled fibres and is acid- and chlorine-free.

GPSR: Easy Access System Europe |
Mustamäe tee 50, 10621 Tallinn, Estonia |
gpsr.requests@easproject.com

The Centre for Literatures in Canada
acknowledges the support of Dr. Eric Schloss
and the Faculty of Arts for the CLC Kreisel
Lecture delivered by David A. Robertson in
March 2025 at the University of Alberta.

University of Alberta Press gratefully
acknowledges the support received for its
publishing program from the Government
of Canada, the Canada Council for the Arts,
and the Government of Alberta through the
Alberta Media Fund.

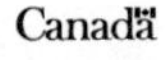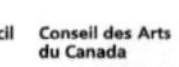

Foreword

For nearly two decades, the Henry Kreisel Memorial Lectures have been making unique contributions to conversations about literary culture in Canada. An annual event in which a distinguished author is invited to explore a topic of deep significance to them as an artist, the Kreisel Lectures offer readers and scholars windows onto what matters to those who are shaping our literatures. By turns polemical, reflective, playful, and scholarly, these lectures range across subjects as diverse as Canadian literary history, Indigenous resurgence, anti-racist poetics, the impact of class on the arts, censorship, and multilingualism. To read these lectures is to get unprecedented insight into what makes these authors tick: their motivations, challenges, preoccupations, and interests. Each one has not only enriched and enlarged our sense of each author and their work, but they have also expanded our understanding of literary life in Canada, remapping its parameters and shading in its intimate textures so that we might be more engaged and informed readers.

David A. Robertson's lecture is the first in this series to foreground the importance of children and youth as readers and agents of social change. That books are too often banned from school libraries (among other places) attests to the power they wield; but, Robertson suggests, the ways that books change us and our communities are different from—and far more positive than—what advocates of book banning fear. As Métis author Conor Kerr underscores in his introduction to Robertson's lecture, seeing yourself and your community depicted in stories *matters*; so too, Robertson adds, does seeing a world enlarged and animated in new ways. An argument for writing not only what you know, but also what you *want* to know, Robertson's lecture turns a spotlight on the next generation and the stories he writes for them as a source of invigorating and healing social change that will ultimately help to build better relationships between Indigenous and non-Indigenous people in Canada.

The book you hold in your hands is the 19th Lecture in the Kreisel Series, which was delivered to a lively audience of readers, educators, and at least one kid, on a chilly spring evening at the University of Alberta in Edmonton / amiskwaciwâskahikan (Treaty 6 territory and Districts 9 and 10 of the Métis Nation of Alberta) in March 2025. The Centre for Literatures in Canada (CLC) is the proud organizer, host, and co-publisher of the lecture series, which is published by University of Alberta Press.

The CLC was established in 2006 thanks to the leadership gift of the noted Edmontonian bibliophile and comics collector, Dr. Eric Schloss. In 2007 this lecture series was established in honour of Professor Henry Kreisel. Author, University Professor, and Officer of the Order of Canada, Kreisel was born into a Jewish family in Vienna in 1922. He left his homeland for England in 1938 and was interned in Canada for eighteen months during the Second World War. After studying at the University of Toronto, he was hired in 1947 to teach at the

University of Alberta, where he was the Chair of English from 1961 to 1970. He served as Vice-President (Academic) from 1970 to 1975, when he was named University Professor, the highest scholarly award bestowed on its faculty members by the University of Alberta. An inspiring and beloved teacher who taught generations of students to appreciate literature, Professor Kreisel was among the first to champion Canadian literature in university classrooms and, through his own writing, to bring the experience of immigrants to modern Canadian literature. Kreisel was also an early advocate for Indigenous research and scholarship at the University of Alberta, working to build bridges between Indigenous communities and the university. His written works include two novels, *The Rich Man* (1948) and *The Betrayal* (1964), and a collection of short stories, *The Almost Meeting* (1981). His internment diary, alongside critical essays on his writing, appears in *Another Country: Writings by and about Henry Kreisel* (1985). He died in Edmonton in 1991. The generosity and foresight of Professor Kreisel's teaching at the University of Alberta continues to inspire the CLC in its research pursuits, public outreach, and ongoing commitment to the ever-growing richness, complexity, and diversity of literatures in Canada.

Sarah Wylie Krotz
June 30, 2025

Introduction

CONOR KERR

My Grandmother's name is Pat Kerr, before she was married it was Pat Ginther. She's a proud Métis woman who is descended from the Métis communities around Edmonton as well as the Papaschase Cree Nation whose land we are currently on right now. Land that was illegally surrendered officially in 1888 even after her great-grandfather, a man named John Quinn Gladue, under the guidance of the matriarchs, negotiated and signed an adhesion to Treaty 6. My Grandmother was raised by her Grandmother, affectionately known in our family as Granny, on road allowances north of St. Paul, Alberta. Granny was born on the Papaschase Cree Nation and left as a young woman when government officials killed their livestock and dogs, and burned down their houses to make way for what would become Strathcona. My Grandmother was raised by Granny and learned the stories of this land. Granny would tell her about how her umbilical cord is buried right where the Low Level Bridge is now. She would tell her about which trails had the best Saskatoon bushes. She talked about how the Millcreek Ravine would echo throughout the nights with fiddle music and drums as people gathered. She talked about how much landscapes, home, community, and pride in who you are, where you come from, and who your community is means everything. As we sit here today, on lands that Indigenous communities have called home forever, I want us to honour their stories, their laughter that echoes through the river valley, their tears and joy that the North Saskatchewan carries forever east. Let's honour that. Acknowledge that. And think about it as we move through our daily lives.

I was raised by my Grandmother and she taught me from a young age to be proud to be Métis. She taught me our family history, our family story, and what it means to hold relationships and culture near to your heart. Not that many kids my age had that same opportunity. In the late 1990s, when I was a kid, we'd drive from Buffalo Pound Lake to Moose Jaw or Saskatoon and I'd get dropped off at the library. I remember looking for characters and stories that resembled me or my friends and the communities that we came from. And there wasn't much out there. There were no graphic novels, or children's books, young adult fiction, or anything like that. Grey Owl might have been the closest thing that you could find.

Holy, do I wish that I had been hitting up that library in Moose Jaw now. Over the past fifteen years, David Robertson has written over twenty-five books across multiple genres including non-fiction, children's and young adult books, and novels. I'm not going to lie, I was initially planning on listing them all out, but that would have taken half the lecture. So I'll just list a couple of my personal favourites, which include the Governor General Award–winning *When We Were Alone*, the Carol Shields Winnipeg Book Award–winning *Black Water: Family, Legacy and Blood Memory*, the Reckoner Rises Series, and The Misewa Saga, the novel *Theory of Crows* and the Governor General Award–winning *On The Trapline*.

To say that David Robertson is prolific is an understatement. He has created in a short period of time an entire canon for Indigenous and non-Indigenous youth and adults across the country to learn more about colonialism, foster care, residential schools, reconciliation, mental health, and their effects on Indigenous kids and families. These are hard topics to discuss. It takes a lot of courage to approach them and it would be easy to dwell on the negative, but one thing about David's writing is that he approaches it from a place of strength.

The legendary Haisla/Heitsuik writer and Kreisel Lecture alumnus Eden Robinson said of David's book *Black Water*, "When someone lives their life in a good way, the Haisla call them handsome people. David A. Robertson's biography is the perfect example of someone who takes care with his words and speaks respectfully; he tackles identity and racism, family bonds and breaks, with nuance and honesty."[1]

Another Kreisel Lecture alumnus Heather O'Neill said that "he explores Cree values and ideas and their richness and relevance in contemporary life. He does so by taking us through the story of one Indigenous family's journey through the twentieth century in Canada. We are faced with horrors and great loss, but also extraordinary warmth and heroics and a family who refused to ever be defined by anyone but themselves. A wondrous history lesson about love."[2]

Born to educators Donald and Bev, David, a father of five, grew up in Winnipeg and graduated from the University of Winnipeg in 1999. Indigenous worldviews and educational concepts are a constant thread throughout his work where they are situated within a contemporary context. As he stated in an interview with *Quill & Quire,* "We have trauma in our history, in our lives, in our family. But really our story is a story of resiliency and a story of cultural reconnection and a story of love. I feel like that will help people understand what healing really means."[3]

I first met David in June of 2022 in Toronto at the Amazon Canada First Novel Award ceremony. My debut novel, *Avenue of Champions,* had been short-listed for the award and I was attending my first literary event, ever. I had never thought that a book about Métis youth and their experiences growing up in Edmonton would be considered for any national awards, and going to a place like the Globe and Mail building in downtown Toronto was incredibly intimidating. As I walked into the gala, I felt over-whelmed. Here was a community that I would never be a part of. Then I saw David chatting with writers Cherie Dimaline and Joshua Whitehead, and the comfort of knowing that other Indigenous people were there eased my anxiety. I didn't win that award, but being able to meet and talk to a Cree writer from Winnipeg who was part of a community that was shaping a new collective of Indigenous literary works made the night and the trip worth it.

I ran into David again this past fall at Calgary's Wordfest. We talked briefly in the author room as he was grabbing a bite to eat after having spent the entire day talking to kids at schools across Calgary. The night before, he had been on back-to-back panels. I would have been exhausted. David looked excited and told me a brief story about how inspirational the kids were at a junior high he had spoken at earlier that day. How their questions gave him hope for how future generations are seeing relationships with Indigenous Peoples. David's writing and the lectures that he gives consider what an ideal future can look like for both Indigenous and non-Indigenous people on these lands.

I think back to when I was a kid in those libraries in Moose Jaw and Saskatoon and how I would have felt if David's works had been available for me. And I think about how all across this country Indigenous youth are picking up his books and seeing their stories reflected in literature and how they will be proud of who they are and the beautiful families, histories, and communities that they come from. That multi-generational impact is immeasurable.

David was recently named the editorial director of Swift Water Books, an Indigenous Children's Book imprint of Penguin Random House Canada's Tundra Books. The name pays homage to his late father's love of water. In 2023 David was awarded an honorary doctorate in letters by the University of Manitoba. And in May 2025 the University of Lethbridge awarded him an honorary doctor of laws. His most recent work, *All the Little Monsters: How I Learned to Live with Anxiety,* was published in January 2025 by HarperCollins.

It is one of the honours of my life to be able to welcome David A. Robertson, a member of Norway House Cree Nation in beautiful Manitoba, to deliver the 2025 Kreisel Lecture.

Notes

1. "Praise for *Black Water*," David A. Robertson's website, https://www.darobertson.ca/.

2. "Praise for *Black Water*," David A. Robertson's website, https://www.darobertson.ca/.

3. Quoted in Ryan Porter, "David A. Robertson," author profile, *Quill & Quire*, Oct. 2020, https://quillandquire.com/authors/the-prolific-david-a-robertson-on-reconnecting-with-his-cree-heritage-and-paying-tribute-to-his-father/.

Every Story Is a Call to Action

Writing is always an act of hope because it assumes a reader. It assumes a reader in the future. The act of writing and the person reading it are separated by time and space.

—MARGARET ATWOOD
in Erica Wagner, "'Writing Is Always an Act of Hope': Margaret Atwood on The Testaments"

When I made the active decision to become a published author, I wanted to create social change through inspiring action.

I envisioned my books being taught in classrooms and stocked on library shelves; I didn't much care for mass market success. Don't get me wrong, being able to put food on the table for my family is something I'm grateful for (and to pay for hockey and school and dance and hockey…did I mention hockey?), but I never expected to get to where I am today. What I did expect was to make a difference in some small manner.

I attribute that expectation to the influence of my father. For decades, he worked in the field of Indigenous Education and was a trailblazer. An innovator. The stuff we are working towards today in the field of education, or what we recognize as necessities but still haven't developed and imple-mented for the success of Indigenous youth in remote and urban locations, he was talking and writing about in the early 1990s. I carry an essay he wrote called "Speaking in Tongues" wherever I go.

Here's a brief excerpt:

The education system has improved with some cultures. For example, a teacher can no longer "stand in front" of French students and teach in English unless they are teaching English. The

Education System has taken the language of the
French people and their culture into consideration,
and they cannot teach without including the
student's culture and experience. What about
the Cree people? Can the teachers stand in front
of the Cree student without knowledge of the
student's language, culture, and experience?
The reality is that Educational Institutions have
not taken the experiences of the Crees into
consideration. Cree language and culture are not
required for certification or teaching in schools—
urban, rural, northern, or Indigenous.[1]

My father was Cree, thus his specificity of Cree
people in his writing, but you can extrapolate this
into any Indigenous group across Turtle Island.
Indigenous people are not given the same consideration as other people, and have been treated, and
still are treated, like second-class citizens.

Years ago, I asked Dad why he didn't take better-
paying jobs, or why he'd never accepted one of many
invitations to run for a political party. He told me
that he only took jobs that would enable him to help
the most people—money or notoriety was never
considered. And certainly not politics. If anything,
notoriety was helpful as a way for him to work from
a bigger platform and positively affect even more
people than he would have been able to otherwise. I
try to keep that in mind, too. Especially when I'm at
a school and signing arms and hands and shirts and
hat bills and the soles of shoes and ripped up pieces
of paper, and sometimes even books. It helps keep

my feet on the ground and my head comfortably fitting through doorways. (The only place I ever feel popular is at an educational institution or an education conference, by the way.)

How could I have expected to make a difference in this country that we now call Canada? I wonder if it doesn't sound as though hubris was involved in my ambition. It may sound this way, but it's not. I often quote Edward Everett Hale, an author, historian, and minister: "I am only one, but still I am one, I cannot do everything, but still I can do something, and I can't let the fact that I can't do everything stop me from doing the one thing that I can do."[2] My father had this taped to the inside of the last notebook he kept, and its message is as profound as it is simple. Anybody has the capability of doing something that will make a lasting impact; my chosen instrument of change has most often been literature. Of course, when it comes to altering the way things are, there is an anticipation of resistance. Change can be uncomfortable, but we have to be comfortable with being uncomfortable, rather than allow fear to dictate our actions.

Case in point, several years ago, a handful of my books, all of them graphic novels, among other works by Indigenous creators in various forms and genres, were banned in Alberta. First, throughout the Edmonton Public Schools, and then, I was informed, by the entire province of Alberta through Alberta Education (I was told recently that some of my books are still not recommended for use). In both cases, most of the books that were targeted (I don't use that word frivolously; book bannings are targeted attacks—that's why the vast majority of books that are challenged and eventually banned are from the LGBTQIA2S+ community) were books about and by Indigenous people. In all cases, the rationale behind the decision to ban the books in question was dubious at best, asinine at worst.

For example, my first published books, collected in an omnibus titled *7 Generations: A Plains Cree Saga*, were banned due to an "inaccurate depiction of Indigenous culture" and that it required teachers to have "pre- and post-conversations with students about the impacts and legacy of the Indian Residential School System."[3] I still wonder what it meant that a book by and about Indigenous people could inaccurately depict Indigenous cultures; it's well known that I am Cree, and this particular book detailed a Cree family's intergenerational history. I think what it came down to, and this is conjecture on my part, albeit based on considerable experience, was that the decision makers had a perception of what Indigenous culture was and my book, as well as others, did not fit into that box. As for this nonsense about having pre- and post-conversations? That's a teacher's job when introducing literature to a class, and I would hope that most educators would find that reasoning to be insulting. On the part of Alberta Education, a teacher was told to stop using *Betty: The Helen Betty Osborne Story*, a graphic novel about the life and brutal murder of a nineteen-year-old Cree woman from Kinosao Sipi (or Norway House Cree Nation), because it inferred that violence occurred

(I suppose there was a concern about whether the inference of violence was appropriate for students— I would say that's entirely dependent on the age of the student and how effectively they've been prepared to process the reality of, in this case, Betty's murder) and that the author (me) was problematic. I have never known what was meant by that assertion. A best guess is that my speaking out about book bannings contributed to decisions that got my book banned. Part of the frustration of this incident was the lack of communication and refusal to provide clarification on the part of the government department.

More recently, a school board in Ontario, the Durham District School Board, pulled three books off shelves and out of classrooms, circumventing their policy to address book challenges to begin with (they asked that I refer to their Indigenous policy, which, in turn, referred me back to the division policy), including *The Great Bear*. Their reasoning stood up to scrutiny about as well as Edmonton's and Alberta's, and frankly, as well as almost any book challenge. That's because book challenges often come from parents and grandparents who don't bother to even read the title in question. In the case of books about or from the LGBTQIA2S+ community, they see the word *gay* and think, "Oh no, not on my watch!" without bothering to read the actual words. And by the way, challenging books by marginalized authors doesn't erase the fact that marginalized people live in our communities, that they are a part of our communities. They erase marginalized people in the same way that tearing down a statue to honour an architect of genocide erases history.

The primary reason for banning *The Great Bear* was that it was the school board's policy not to teach culture. What the school board failed to recognize, or willfully ignored, was that all books are culture. The Durham District School Board's policy, it seems, was not to teach *some* culture. Books, all books, are keepers of cultural heritage and history. They hold collective wisdom, traditions, and stories within their pages that span generations. They are iconic cultural entities, and seeing them for what they are allows us to capture and preserve their intrinsic and lasting value. Stories are forever—the wisdom my father gifted me with has been gifted to my children, and that cycle will continue. Stories are forever unless we allow them to be snuffed out by hate and ignorance.

If it's true that all stories are culture, it's not a stretch to hold as a truth that all stories are, as well, political. If books, if stories, are keepers of cultural heritage and history, they are also inherently political. Stories are the expression of one's beliefs or ideology to somebody else. In the case of books, that *somebody else* is the reader: the consumer of the words that have been placed onto the page with great care, precision, and thought. Stories are a gift. They transfer knowledge from one to another. The reader processes the information with which they have been gifted. If the storytelling is compelling, concise, creative, and relevant, the reader cannot help but be changed and, what's more, motivated by it.

I'm going to talk about reconciliation a lot in this lecture. I think it's inevitable, given my line of work. I will also break down the term to better articulate what sort of activism writing can inspire, because you cannot act effectively on something that is a misnomer—but hold on a paragraph or two for that, if you don't mind indulging me.

Now, my father, as well as being Dad, was my best friend, role model, mentor, and hero. I do everything I do because of the example he set for me in his work. Sometimes, our work intersected. We would find each other at the same conference. We would go for lunch together, or take turns watching each other present, me on something to do with books, and Dad with something to do with education. Of course, the two can be synonymous—books should educate as much as they should entertain. That's why my father's teachings hit so hard and so effectively: What he told me about his focus in the work he did was what I saw in my focus as an author, and eventually, the other sandboxes I would play in as a freelance journalist, podcaster, public speaker, and editorial director of my imprint with Penguin Random House Canada, Swift Water Books.

It should come as no surprise that he and I spoke often of reconciliation. We both appreciated concision. Say what you're going to say in as few words as possible. By the way, I know that's not what you're getting here, but you'll have to forgive me this deviation. What was the simplest way to describe the act of reconciliation? Well, it was a process of communication for both of us. It was two people sitting across from one another, or one person standing in front of several people, and having a conversation. The trick is to do so without any inherent bias, something that we all carry with us, whether we'd like to admit it or not. So, we see through all the preconceptions, all the luggage that we carry with us (i.e., an Indigenous person will probably wear moccasins, have their hair braided, may talk in that familiar rez accent, be stoic, and so on), push all of it aside, to see each other as human beings and connect on that level in one thing that we all share: the human condition. We have all experienced love, loss, joy, and grief. We can also have shared values, even if we present them differently.

The more we understand what brings us together, the more we learn about what our differences are and work to see them through this clear lens, the better we can envision where we have been, where we are because of it, and where we need to go in order to live well with each other in a stronger and safer community. Where the success of one contributes to the success of all. You cannot fix a problem unless you know there is one, and you have a good understanding of what the barriers are; that's how you break those barriers down.

Just as we share so much in being human, in living with the human condition, stories also share things. Every single form of writing—from books in all their forms and genres (picture books, graphic novels, poetry, novels, fiction, non-fiction, historical fiction, fantasy, sci-fi, horror, short stories, flash fiction, memoir), to blogs, to social media posts, to articles and op-eds, to Saturday morning comics to journals to speeches to translations to emails—is distinct. Still, they disseminate one thing, if only one thing, and that is knowledge transfer.

My biography used to say this, and because what you write is forever, I still hear it a lot when I'm introduced: "David writes books that educate as much as they entertain." This is true. Stories can do both; they should do both, and even more. Stories reveal the world around us, in all of its beauty and all of its warts, in all of the challenges we face— in the successes we achieve by overcoming those challenges, and in the failures we experience and what we learn from those failures when we do not overcome the challenges we are presented with. Stories reveal the world around us and, more than that, articulate our place in it. Stories provide commentary on historical and contemporary events to better understand where we are from and where we have been. If you have that awareness, you have been gifted it, in some way, through Story. So, all stories are political, and within the context of this conversation, all stories are, as well, a call to action.

This is why stories, books, and writing are a form of activism. That is why when you write a story, you should accept the responsibility of the activism they encourage. Activism requires intention and its resultant action, or else we cannot call it activism at all. Calls for change change nothing unless action follows. This is why one of the first things I wanted to dive into is those who would silence the very tools of activism, tools that influence, inspire, and motivate our most vital agents of change.

In my earlier discussion on book bannings, I mentioned how the school board in question had established a policy to handle book challenges, which people have a right to do. You can challenge a book, even if the reasons are ignorant and uninformed. Dave Levithan wrote a book called *Answers in the Pages* that addressed book bannings of stories about and by the LGBTQIA2S+ community. In the book, a parent reads the last paragraph of a book where two boys hug. That's it. All they do is hug. And based on that very gay action (the boys are gay, but so what? I hug everybody all the time), the parent, a mother in this case, initiates a challenge that leads to the book being pulled from classrooms. What Levithan gives us in the book is the ability to read the story that was banned, and not just the last paragraph. It provides much-needed context, which the parent *should have* bothered to gather. It's a coming-of-age adventure story where two characters, boys, happen to have feelings for each other. Levithan offers a roadmap to consider how policy can better handle book challenges. In this case, it begs the question, What does policy do when books are challenged, and what does it truly protect?

Parents or grandparents who lead calls to challenge books by marginalized groups might say that these stories protect their children from indoctrination, as though a novel can make you gay. As far as I know, if you're gay, you're gay. It's like when I asked my father, years ago, why he didn't teach me how to be Cree. In response, he asked me, "How am I going to teach you how to be Cree?" Following that same logic, how can you teach somebody to be gay? You can't. You are either gay or you are not gay. Period. You don't choose to be gay as much as somebody chooses to be straight. Calls to ban books are ostensibly done to "protect children," but do children need to be protected when it comes to books? Does it protect a child to ignore people who live in their community? Does it protect anybody to ignore the existence of human beings who live with us in our communities? I would argue that it does exactly the opposite, that it harms us, and it certainly harms children, to take stories away. No, children don't need to be protected. They're doing just fine, and their empathy and acceptance are things we can all learn from. A policy that addresses book challenges should not be focused on protecting children; it should be put in place to protect books.

Writing in any shape that addresses policy or motivates some action that can lead to change is critical for reaching the ultimate goal of reform in their respective calls for action.

I write a lot from lived experience. The focus of my writing has always been activism, and with each story I write, I ask myself the same question. The question is a litmus test for whether I move forward with a story or if I leave it on the cutting room floor. I ask myself not only if what I am writing is a good story, but, almost more importantly, whether or not it can help to create meaningful change. I don't move forward with it if it cannot do so, even if I feel that it's a great concept. That's why I can confidently say that every single book I've written, every single podcast script I've developed, every article I've taken on, and every story I've told in person has had the goal of creating social change. We all should have a similar goal, no matter what discipline we choose to work in.

The prospect of creating any measurable change is daunting. We have to have a vision of a long-term impact. My father used to tell me that any change he sought to achieve was something he wouldn't see in his lifetime. I saw this was true after his death. He worked in Indigenous Education, as I've mentioned. The main area of focus for him was to build up the capacity for First Nations communities to have what he called Local Control, to be able to teach their kids with autonomy and agency by themselves, and without any outside interference. He developed teacher training programs to accomplish this, the most significant of which was likely BUNTEP (Brandon University Northern Teachers Education Program), which is still running today out of UCN (University College of the North),[4] a post-secondary institution that was a dream of his and which he chaired the implementation of as the first Indigenous chair of the Council on Post-Secondary Education in Manitoba. After his death, I was giving a keynote address to a room full of Indigenous educators in the Canadian Museum for Human Rights at The Forks in Winnipeg. After the session, many teachers approached me. For the most part, they did not approach me about the session I had just delivered, but rather to tell me how my father's work had helped them. In that moment, I saw exactly what my father had meant.

I know the prospect can be daunting because there's so much to be done in so little time. After all, most of us consider life to be short. Sure, in the grand scheme of things, it is. But I wonder if, in the case of taking action that leads to change, the idiom is entirely accurate. Another role I have taken on is being a mental health advocate. As somebody who lives with mental health struggles, I often turn to videos that I feel have value in imparting wisdom that I can learn from, and that I, in turn, can use in my work. I watch a video of Tony Robbins often, because not only is it useful, but it always makes me cry (I like to cry; my father told me that tears are important, that they are pain and grief and trauma leaving the body). In the clip, he tells an audience member, who reports to be suicidal, that you overestimate what you can do in a year, but you underestimate what you can do in two or three decades.[5] There's time.

I love public speaking. As somebody who lives with depression and anxiety, that might sound odd. When discussing, generally, people's worst fears, public speaking often ranks a shade below death. But I have always found it calming. Even though I can't quite put a finger on it, I know that when I'm on stage in front of people, it relaxes me—maybe it's a distraction from my typical worries. I give talks on a variety of subjects. They're usually about

Indigenous people, historical and contemporary issues, reconciliation, one of my books, or mental health, as I've grown to become more of an advocate year over year. I love doing all of these presentations. The only thing I kind of don't love is offering writing workshops—I don't know how to articulate what I do, and I'm not even convinced that I do it all that well. The little monster on my shoulder, one of many little monsters that mental health spawns, continually tells me that I've no business teaching somebody else anything about writing, though objectively, I've done okay at the profession. It's a lifelong impostor syndrome. But I agree to workshops here and there, and I do find that writing workshops have allowed me to identify and refine my writing process.

Despite not feeling as if I know a lot about writing, I do know one or two things.

Write what you know.

That's a terrible piece of advice that new and emerging writers get regularly. Now, there's a place for writing what you know. I incorporate what I know into setting quite often. Many of my stories take place in Winnipeg and Norway House Cree Nation. In The Misewa Saga series, Morgan and Eli live in a foster home that used to be a house I lived in. They go to River Heights Middle School, and so did I. In this way, writing what you know helps to provide authenticity. Authenticity leads to believability, and that brand of engagement leads, in turn, to immersion in the story. Of course, that's not all that leads to immersion and engagement, but it plays a part.

But you can't only write what you know. We read to learn, and if we read to learn, we certainly write to learn. I have always believed that writing is a practice of exploration. Don't write what you know, but rather write what you want to know. Write to understand the world and your place in it. And yes, write to understand how you can be an active participant in the pursuit of social change, to leave this world better than when you came into it. And if you write what you *want to know*, if you write what you *are passionate about*, you will, in turn, figure out what you *ought to do*.

It'll be different from what I feel I ought to do, and that's a good thing. We can't all take the same action, and we can't all have the same goals. Even if we are all concerned with reconciliation, which is a good objective to have, which is a good "ought to do," there is an abundance of roles that we can play to ensure that we get to where we need to go, to find ourselves in a place of healing and community.

Whatever you decide your role can be, I can say that Story plays a part, either in the actions that we take, or how we decide what actions we should take. I wonder if you wouldn't humour me in breaking down, as a case study, what I'm talking about. In the process, maybe selfishly, it will give you motivation and a bit of guidance, through Story, to walk this path with Indigenous people.

Surely, the road to reconciliation is paved with Story. The phrase *Truth and Reconciliation* means the two are inextricably linked—reconciliation and truth. While the definition and understanding of what reconciliation means and what it entails are up for discussion, at its most basic, albeit still complex form, it is the act of building community. Truth means what *really* happened and what is *still* happening across Turtle Island. For too long, our stories, as Indigenous Peoples, have been told by others. Only recently, within the last fifteen years, have we begun to reclaim our truth and share it with others through Story. This has created a revolutionary change that has ripped apart the fabric of what we thought this country was, and has stitched together a new understanding of what this country *is*. It also gives us a clearer vision of what this country *can be*. I was asked recently at a book launch, "What is the legacy of this country?" and my answer was that the legacy is what we make it. We haven't developed our legacy yet, and that's what the work is. What do we want our legacy to be? We have the legacy that we have now, but we have a lot of work to do yet, and we have an opportunity to change what that legacy is. Everybody needs to develop a vision of what we can be, as opposed to what we are now.

But let's back up a moment. In the interest of continuing to have a fulsome, in-depth conversation, let's look at the word *reconciliation* and consider whether or not this is what we are trying to do. If, on this journey, we are seeking to reconcile. After all, how can we accomplish something if we don't truly understand what it is? We may as well try to thrust a hammer into wood with a nail.

The act of reconciliation, according to the dictionary, is the restoration of friendly relations. What is an example of true reconciliation? Well, when we consider reconciliation, there needs to be acknowledgement not only of the roles we can play, but the differing roles that exist between non-Indigenous and Indigenous people. A few years ago, the day after the acquittal of the man accused of murdering Tina Fontaine, I was in Kinosao Sipi doing a few days' worth of school visits at the Helen Betty Osborne Ininiw Education Resource Centre and Jack River School. At Jack River School, I spoke with elementary school children. In the middle of the day, I was having lunch with the principal at the time, and she told me children and adults in the community were still broken. "You can't heal brokenness with brokenness," she told me, and I've thought a lot about that since. The principal was correct. In many First Nations communities, a lot of people are still broken or breaking from the profound impact of colonialism. We have healing to do, individually, within families, and in our communities. Before settlers came to this country and disrupted our ways of living, we were doing just fine, thank you very much. Contrary to the popular attitude towards First Nations people, an attitude held by the most powerful person in this country (Prime Minister John A. Macdonald),[6] we were not at all the savages we were thought to be. But every effort was made, and is still being made, to break us. Despite our resiliency and the hard work of cultural reclamation, people are struggling. We, indeed, are trying our best to restore friendly relations, to return to a right relationship. Healing has occurred and continues to happen, and eventually, generations from now, I believe that we will achieve reconciliation.

Here is my question to you, and yes, it is rhetorical: When were relations between Indigenous and non-Indigenous people friendly? In other words, when was there a *right relationship*? Of course, there was not, and there continues not to be. So, what are we trying to do in this broader scope of reconciliation? I know we don't want to return to anything, because there is nothing worth returning to. Rather, we want to work towards something. We want to build something right for the first time, and then make it sustainable. To do that, we have to reconsider what reconciliation is, if we should even call it that, and what it entails. What stories are we listening to and reading, what are they teaching us, and how are they preparing us? How do these stories motivate us to take actions that lead to change?

When I was younger, I was disconnected from my identity as a Cree person. There were a lot of factors that led to this. My grandmother was a residential school survivor and died without sharing her story; survivors weren't supported and didn't feel safe to share their experiences back then, and that will always be a lost history. I've learned what I can about Norway House Indian Residential School, but I have not found much specific information about my grandmother except for a couple of records and photographs. Indian Residential School history was not taught in schools in the 1980s (or in the '90s, really, for that matter...or not widely at all until the 2010s), and I didn't learn about residential schools until I was out of high school. There was an Indian Residential School, Assiniboia Residential School, down the street from Kelvin High School. Assiniboia Residential School was a place where friends of mine, some alive and some who have now passed on, attended, and as high school students in a place of education, we never knew that building was there, let alone the history of it. What a failure! And an *accurate* representation of Indigenous Peoples in popular culture, including literature? Forget it. All I recall seeing were the tropes so commonly associated with Indigenous people—stereotypes like the savage or noble Indian. I never saw anything that represented true Indigeneity. The first book I ever read about Indigenous people by an Indigenous person was *April Raintree* by Beatrice Mosionier. My *coming to* as a Cree person was enabled by Story: what I learned from my father and his contemporaries, after my father's reconciliation with my mother, and the modest and modestly increasing number of books that were being written about Indigenous people *by* Indigenous people.

Stories, then, are what had an impact on me. They were, in written and oral form, what not only taught me about who I was, who I am, as a Cree person, but what I needed to do to ensure that what I did helped the most people. That what I *could* do, I *ought* to do, even if I were only one person.

I mentioned earlier that you should write what you want to know, and that you should try to understand the world and your place in it. That applies here. The greatest gift in my writing and advocacy has been the knowledge that I have sought out or have been given, and it's a journey I will always be on, because there will always be more to learn. *7 Generations: A Plains Cree Saga* is a story about a teenage boy named Edwin who is struggling with mental health to such an extent that he attempts to die by suicide. His mother finds him in time to save his life, but realizes that he's still broken. She tells him the story of his family, going back about 150 years. The last two issues of the collection discuss almost exclusively Indian Residential Schools and intergenerational trauma.

Though my early focus was narrow (my next book, *Sugar Falls*, was also about the legacy of Indian Residential Schools), I learned something valuable that I have carried with me for my entire career and all the roles I have taken on and accepted. If you see something is wrong and you have the capacity to make it right, then you have a *responsibility* to make it right. If you see something is missing, that there is a gap that needs to be filled, and you have the ability, then you must fill that gap. Even if people tell you that it cannot be done, they often believe that only because it has not been done *yet*.

My first picture book encompasses this truth. I wrote *When We Were Alone* after reading through the Truth and Reconciliation Commission's Calls to Action, which stated that Indian Residential School history needed to be taught from kindergarten through high school. By that time, I had seen the transformative power of literature when used in an educational setting, but there wasn't a book about the Indian Residential School system for readers that young. I knew that I could write a picture book. I'd read hundreds upon hundreds of them, and my first love was poetry; the best picture books incorporate a poet's sensibility. I recognized the gap: There were no picture books for kindergarteners about the Indian Residential School system. And even though I was told that the topic was too complex and too sensitive for young readers, I believed there was an approach that would work, that didn't traumatize kids, but instead informed them and built within them the most powerful emotion of all: empathy. In short, it could be done; it just hadn't been done *yet*. *When We Were Alone* went on to win a Governor General's Literary

Award, but far more importantly, it is still used in classrooms today to teach young learners about the Indian Residential School system.

What I have come to understand, through lived experience, in the books I have published, and in the communities I have been fortunate enough to visit, is that reconciliation encompasses more than the Indian Residential School system. Of course, residential schools will always be at the heart of reconciliation, but it is also one of several systems that have negatively impacted Indigenous people, families, and communities. It is one of several colonial systems that caused the brokenness I wrote of earlier.

At times, the effect of these systems is subtle. It is not readily visible. But still, it's there. My father grew up on a trapline. He was born in 1935, and from 1935, when he was as young as six months old, he spent most of his time on the land. That was where he lived, played, worked, and learned (through Story and by doing). It was a beautiful way to live, but that way of life was cut short in 1945, when he was ten years old, by the government's first social assistance program. Why is this system colonial, and how did it disproportionately affect Indigenous people? The social assistance program required families who opted to receive monetary support to live at a fixed address. This meant that families who lived on the land had to choose, because there were no fixed addresses on traplines, and many chose to leave that way of life behind. My father said that it "broke up the trap for many people." The program also required children to attend school. For Indigenous children, this meant that they would either attend an Indian Residential School or a Day School. My father was a Day School survivor, an experience that led him to eventually write the paper I quoted from earlier: "Speaking in Tongues."

My father writes,

> The door opened to the building and a small, untanned person walked into the room, walked in front of everybody and began to speak in "tongues." (This is a term I learned later in life.) She was very confident and commanded respect from the young people; some of the young people appeared to respond in the same strange sounds she was making. I was nine years old, an adult in the eyes of my people, and I did not understand the words she was making. I became very scared and insecure. In one brief session, in the small one-room classroom, I had lost confidence and became confused about the learning situation.[7]

The systems and epidemics that have traumatized and marginalized Indigenous people are profound and far-reaching. They can be traced back centuries. Many of them are still operating today, and the effect on Indigenous communities will be felt for generations to come. This includes the foster care system. When I visit schools, I ask children to put up their hands if they have learned about the Indian Residential School system. Every single child puts their hand up. It tells me that we have made progress. Then I ask them to put up their hands if they have learned about the foster care system. I rarely see any hands reaching into the air. We aren't doing enough, and that is not an indictment. We simply have to do more. We have to learn and, in turn, teach youth about the Sixties Scoop. How, even today, the foster care system may be doing as much damage as the Indian Residential School system did.

Consider this: There are more Indigenous children in foster care today than at the peak of the Indian Residential School system. Out of all children in foster care, almost 55 per cent of those children are Indigenous, while in Canada, Indigenous children account for under 8 per cent of all kids under the age of 15.[8] Overrepresentation and mistreatment can be seen time and time again in the justice system, where in 2022–23, Indigenous adults made up 30 per cent of admissions to correctional services, and Indigenous women were incarcerated at a rate 15.4 times higher than non-Indigenous women.[9] What are the causes for this? Marginalization, systemic discrimination, and colonialism.

The grandparents, who my father called Elders, will say that healing from the intergenerational impacts of trauma will take seven generations, but the reality is that the clock hasn't started ticking yet—trauma is still occurring. We're doing the same things today that we were doing one hundred years ago.

The health care system does not have equitable access or treatment for Indigenous people. Brian

Sinclair and my auntie, Olive Kirkness, died because they were left for too long in an emergency room in Winnipeg, and in 2020, in Quebec, Joyce Echaquan was laughed at and belittled by hospital staff while she died *in their care*. Access continues to be a problem in the education system, where many Indigenous children still need to leave home to achieve what is a human right: the ability to attain a secondary degree.

We have epidemics like MMIWG2S (Missing and Murdered Indigenous Women, Girls, and Two-Spirit People). Let me run down some quick stats for you, but ones that we all should know. Indigenous women are four times more likely than non-Indigenous women to be victims of violence. They are twice as likely to experience violence from their current or former partner. They are more likely to experience physical and sexual assault than non-Indigenous women. From 2001 to 2014, the average rate of homicides involving Indigenous female victims was four times that of those involving non-Indigenous female victims. Indigenous women are twelve times more likely to be murdered or go missing than any other group of women in Canada.[10] The government has rightly called the epidemic a genocide. There is also an epidemic of suicide rates among Indigenous people, where the rate is three times higher than the non-Indigenous population, and on-reserve, the suicide rate is twice as high as Indigenous people living off-reserve (rates vary from community to community, of course).[11] Stop me if you've heard this, but the high rates of suicide can be linked to discrimination, loss of culture and language, and the pervasive consequences of colonialism.

How are we going to heal? How are we going to achieve reconciliation, heal ourselves, build good relationships, and reach equitable treatment because we recognize that the success of one person in our community is the success of many? How are we going to walk this path together? These are loaded questions, and I recognize that. But fixing the problems that colonialism has inflicted upon Indigenous communities first requires us to recognize there are problems to begin with, and what those problems are. We learn from the power of Story, and we are called to action by the knowledge we are gifted with through Story. In writing our stories, in listening to the stories that have been shared and what they have to offer, we learn that what we're talking about here, what we want to see in the future we want to build, is not only about trauma. Yes, there has been suffering, there is no denying that, but there has been, and is, great beauty, too.

There are transformative moments of reclamation. We are taking back our histories in what my friend Richard Van Camp has called a renaissance of Indigenous storytelling. We are telling stories that, for so long, were told by others, stories from our own lived experiences. This has contributed, and continues to contribute, to the truth when we discuss Truth and Reconciliation. Writing our truths is a form of activism because people know they should be entitled to the truth. Not some alternate version of the truth that attempts to placate, in this case, Canadians, with empty and tired rhetoric. Always look for literature from lived experience, but an expansive experience that concerns itself not just with trauma but with a land-based focus—of environmental protection and land stewardship, with language revitalization, because we know that language is our strongest tie to culture and, when we lose it, we lose a part of who we are as Indigenous people. That's why in all of my books now I include the Swampy Cree dialect, because every time I do, I like to think that there is at least one kid who sees their language and feels empowered and encouraged to learn it; we are losing the speakers and it is an area of desperate concern. When my father died, the language died in our family because, due to the impacts of colonialism, of my father's experience in Day School and my grandmother's at Norway House Indian Residential School, my brothers and I were never taught. It was my father's only regret. Look for literature that concerns itself with cultural preservation, with community, with our values, beliefs, and traditions. Not only so that other people understand, appreciate, and respect our differing ways of living and knowing across the many Indigenous cultures on Turtle Island, but so we can hold onto them with a sure and steady grip. Seek out literature that concerns itself with representation and its many levels, and not only accurate, authentic representation of Indigenous Peoples across Turtle Island in the writing that we offer, which leads to empowerment for Indigenous people and knowledge and resultant action for non-Indigenous people, but advocates for the visibility of Indigenous, BIPOC, and LGBTQIA2S+ writers in the classroom.

I cannot tell you how important it is to give us the platform, the space, and the time to tell our stories. I cannot tell you how important it is to invite me out to a high-profile lecture like the Kreisel, or my best friend, Cherie Dimaline, who stole my topic of mental health a few years ago (totally kidding; *An Anthology of Monsters* is beautiful and vital). The *visibility* of marginalized authors, of successful Indigenous people, crushes stereotypes and preconceptions that, let's not fool ourselves, are still prevalent today. As one example, there is a perception that Indigenous people are lazy, that we are every bit the tired stereotype that has been ingrained into the public consciousness through years of bombardment. But how does that opinion shift if you know that from January to June 2025, I didn't spend more than a few weeks at home because I was on the road supporting my work, but more importantly, supporting my family? Or when somebody like Cherie Dimaline is right there in front of a crowd, rapt in attention? A national bestseller for around seven years straight, a Governor General's Literary Award–winner, a Kirkus Prize winner, the Writers' Trust Engel Findley Award–winner, and somebody hard to get a hold of because she's busy in the writing room with Brit Marling, working on a Netflix show called *A Murder At the End of the World*, or creating a prequel for *IT* that tells the backstory of Pennywise. She, like so many Indigenous artists today, is killing it.

Representation extends beyond marginalized voices, beyond the visibility of those voices, into, as we are all aware, because of Cherie's excellent lecture here just a couple of years ago, mental health awareness, an epidemic that desperately requires the kind of action that can be initiated through the power of storytelling. Now, I don't want to tread on a path that has already been walked on by steady feet, but what I can say, as an example of the power of this brand of representation, is that after my memoir on mental health, *All the Little Monsters*, came out, by May 2025, I received approximately one hundred messages from people who had read it, and who had all, in some way, been called into action, either for themselves or for others. Why? Because they saw themselves reflected in a book.

One of those messages read, "Just finished *All the Little Monsters*. I didn't realize the extent to which I have anxiety. Your book brought me to several realizations and has gotten me to seek help for my anxiety. Still in the very beginning stages…but I do believe you have transformed my life and changed the path in which I was heading." Accurate, representative literature should be a human right.

Everybody deserves the ability and access to see themselves in a story or learn about the lives of others who live in this community with us, which leads to understanding, love, and respect. It reminds me of a teaching my father gave me. It is a Cree teaching called non-interference. You don't interfere with how another person lives. Rather, you model what it means to live a good life and what it means to *seek* a good life. What in Cree and Anishinaabemowin is called mino-pimatisiwin. The Good Life. What greater action can there be? How much more effective can activism be than building a community based on these principles: love, understanding, respect, and acceptance?

The actions of one turn into the actions of many. I often think of the starfish analogy, which originates from "The Star Thrower," by Loren Eiseley, first published in 1969. There is a boy on the beach filled with starfish that have been brought in with the tide and left to die. The boy is throwing the starfish into the water, one after the other. It is an impossible task, given that he is but one on a beach full of sea creatures. An older man asks the boy why he's doing it, because he can't possibly make a difference with all the starfish there on the beach. The boy throws another starfish into the ocean and says that he made a difference to that one. There is more to the story, though. At least, I like to imagine there is. After seeing the boy doing this work, the old man joins in. Upon seeing the two folks throwing starfish into the ocean, a crowd of onlookers on the beach contribute to the cause, and soon, there is a community of people taking part. By the end of the day, there is not one starfish left.

Who were those people who helped the boy throw the starfish back into the ocean? Well, social activism is not just *what* you write about, not just the stories you tell, but who you are writing for.

When I decided what I wanted to write about and what I wanted to help change, I also had to decide who I would fight for and with. I had to decide who my agents of change would be in this work of social activism. I asked myself, in the decision-making process, "What segment of the population has the greatest capacity, who has the best chance to create meaningful and lasting social change?"

The answer was self-evident. The answer has always been youth. While writing may not provide the same immediate impact as a protest or a demonstration, while it may lack a similar sense of urgency in that immediacy, it compensates with an ability to reach a wide audience, and its effectiveness as a method of activism exists within the audience you choose to consider.

Children are willing to open themselves up to *experiences*. We aren't. Adults always say they want to protect children, but they're protecting themselves. Besides, when it comes to stories—I know I've said this before, but it bears repeating—you can't, and shouldn't, protect children. They know everything already. They *unlearn* things with an adult's particular brand of protection. Their protection is interference.

Words, in a written or oral form, are permanent. I often think of the story I based my fantasy novel, *The Barren Grounds*, on: ochekatchakosuk, or the fisher stars constellation—more commonly known as the Big Dipper. It's an old story—how old, I'm not certain—but older than the story most people think *The Barren Grounds* is based on: *The Lion, The Witch, and The Wardrobe*. Time has no hold over it. In fact, from wherever that story originated, if anything, this traditional story, among many others, has broadened its reach. In researching constellation stories, I found multiple versions across geographical areas and throughout many differing Indigenous cultural groups. Stories don't die, and so the messages held within them don't either. Words, then, overcome environmental and situational barriers to capture the receiver's attention, encouraging them, through engagement, to pause and reflect on the ideas conveyed. The meaning between the lines. And there is no segment of the population more adept at pulling meaning from between the lines than children. Maurice Sendak, one of my literary heroes, said once of youth, "I don't believe that there's a demarcation. 'Oh, you mustn't tell them that. You mustn't tell them that.' You tell them anything you want. You tell them if it's true. If it's true, you tell them."[12] Sendak said that adults read at more of a surface level, if they read anything at all (case in point, book challenges), while children dig in. They dig in and they uncover meaning. They don't just read between the lines; they burrow in and excavate lessons inherent in stories. The activism they are, and the activism that they promote. On a hot summer day in 2021, my family and I were driving to the Manitoba Legislative Building for a protest following the "discovery" of unmarked graves at Indian Residential School sites in British Columbia and Saskatchewan. En route, we heard about a girl, Willa, who had set up a lemonade stand to raise money to support Indian Residential School survivors. We took a detour and bought lemonade from Willa, along with several other people who had lined up for a cold drink and, more importantly, a good cause. The following day, we learned that Willa had raised over a thousand dollars, which she donated to the Indian Residential School Survivors Society and Mama Bear Clan. At the time, Willa was nine years old. In a social media post, Willa's mother explained that she had learned the history, it had upset her, and she wanted to do something about it.

She did.

Children have had, in my experience, a tremendous influence, and not only as it relates to residential school history. I have seen what they have done when it comes to book bannings; they have taken it upon themselves in school divisions to rewrite entire land acknowledgements to accurately move from sentiment to intentionality; they led the renaming of a school that used to be Ryerson Elementary— it wasn't the teachers or the parents that led that charge; and when we picture the leaders in environmental protection, who are the first people to come to mind? Political leaders? Adults? No. Autumn Peltier and Greta Thunberg. Youth.

The most important job we have as adults—as parents and teachers—is to equip children with knowledge so they can do the work of social change, to immerse them with Story, with the written and spoken word, from lived experiences, from once-muted marginalized voices, to make better decisions than have been made in the past. And while we're at it, we may just find that we are learning as much as the children we are entrusted to educate. We would do well to rediscover the power of curiosity, respect, and empathy that youth possess. The last two years of my father's life, he told me that he was reclaiming teachings and memories from his youth, things that he had lost in favour of learning English for Day School. To learn in English, he had to *unlearn* what he knew in Swampy Cree. What he reclaimed helped him; it didn't matter that it had been seven decades. In my line of work, I see youth every week, sometimes every day. I think about them often, and it makes me think about my childhood, too. I used to say that kids don't see colour—that might be an idiom, I'm not sure—but that's dismissive of the rich diversity in our communities. And it's not true. The truth is, kids do see colour, they simply don't carry preconceptions about one's appearance unless they are taught to do so. Kids see other kids, just as, in the spirit of reconciliation, when we look at one another, we should first see another human being. It's simple, but, of course, it's not. But what kind of a world would it be if we all conducted ourselves in this way, if we carried this value, like youth do? That's something to strive for. That's something that truly builds community, isn't it?

I carry my father's words and his consideration of the pathway to building a better future. A pathway, like me, he believed to be forged with Story in the hands of the youth.

In terms of looking at the future, we have a responsibility to look at our own seven generations from where we are and to look into the future. We want to look back to see what happened. We want to experience what's happening here and now. But we want to look forward into the future and develop a vision of (it) that will help, that will give us hope, that will give young people hope, that will give children hope, in terms of what it is they want to look forward to.[13]

The future hasn't happened yet. The future will be what we determine it to be in the next seven generations. That's where our control is and where we need to look ahead to. I don't know your role, and even if I did, I wouldn't tell you. Intention and action mean less if it's prescriptive. What I do know is that you have a role. We all do. The beginning of the pathway is figuring out what you can do.

And what you can do, you ought to do.

Notes

1. Donald Robertson, "Speaking in Tongues," unpublished manuscript, 1993.

2. Quoted in Jeanie A.B. Greenough, *A Year of Beautiful Thoughts for Boys and Girls* (G.W. Jacobs & Co., 1902), 172, https://www.loc.gov/item/02026066/.

3. Edmonton Public Schools, "Books to Weed Out," defunct website.

4. BUNTEP is now known as Kenanow Bachelor of Education at the University College of the North.

5. The clip is taken from the Netflix documentary *Tony Robbins: I Am Not Your Guru* (2016), https://www.youtube.com/watch?v=k_YqsqJBUfw&rco=1.

6. Prime Minister Macdonald said, "When the school is on the reserve, the child lives with its parents, who are savages; he is surrounded by savages, and though he may learn to read and write, his habits and training mode of thought are Indian. He is simply a savage who can read and write." From the *Official Report of the Debates of the House of Commons of the Dominion of Canada*, 9 May 1883, p. 1107–1108, https://parl.canadiana.ca/view/oop.debates_HOC0501_02/2.

7. Robertson, "Speaking in Tongues."

8. These data are from the Government of Canada, "Reducing the Number of Indigenous Children in Care," last modified 17 Feb. 2025, https://www.sac-isc.gc.ca/eng/1541187352297/1541187392851.

9. Paul Robinson et al., "Over-Representation of Indigenous Persons in Adult Provisional Custody, 2019/2020 and 2020/2021," Statistics Canada, 12 July 2023, https://www150.statcan.gc.ca/n1/pub/85-002-x/2023001/article/00004-eng.htm.

10. Assembly of First Nations, "Murdered & Missing Indigenous Women & Girls," accessed 25 August 2025, https://afn.ca/rights-justice/murdered-missing-indigenous-women-girls/.

11. Mohan B. Kumar and Michael Tjepkema, "Suicide Among First Nations People, Métis and Inuit (2011–2016): Findings from the 2011 Canadian Census Health and Environment Cohort," Statistics Canada, 28 June 2019, https://www150.statcan.gc.ca/n1/pub/99-011-x/99-011-x2019001-eng.htm.

12. Quoted in the documentary *Tell Them Anything You Want: A Portrait of Maurice Sendak*, directed by Lance Bangs and Spike Jonze (HBO, 2009).

13. Donald Robertson on video, quoted in "Episode 5: The Future," *Kiwew*, 24 July 2025, https://www.cbc.ca/listen/cbc-podcasts/425-kiwew/episode/16159930-episode-5-the-future.

Bibliography

Assembly of First Nations. "Murdered & Missing Indigenous Women & Girls." https://afn.ca/rights-justice/murdered-missing-indigenous-women-girls/. Accessed 25 August 2025.

Bangs, Lance, and Spike Jonze, dirs. *Tell Them Anything You Want: A Portrait of Maurice Sendak*. HBO, 2009.

Berlinger, Joe, dir. *Tony Robbins: I Am Not Your Guru*. 2016. Netflix.

Dimaline, Cherie. *An Anthology of Monsters: How Story Saves Us from Our Anxiety*, U of Alberta P, 2023.

Eiseley, Loren. "The Star Thrower." *The Unexpected Universe*. Harcourt, Brace & World, 1969.

"Episode 5: The Future." *Kiwew*, CBC Podcasts, 24 July 2025, https://www.cbc.ca/listen/cbc-podcasts/425-kiwew/episode/16159930-episode-5-the-future.

Government of Canada. *Official Report of the Debates of the House of Commons of the Dominion of Canada.* 9 May 1883, https://parl.canadiana.ca/view/oop. debates_HOC0501_02/2.

Government of Canada. "Reducing the Number of Indigenous Children in Care." 17 Feb. 2025, https://www.sac-isc.gc.ca/eng/1541187352297/1541187392851.

Greenough, Jeanie A.B. *A Year of Beautiful Thoughts for Boys and Girls.* G.W. Jacobs & Co., 1902, https://www.loc.gov/item/02026066/.

Holland, Bernard. "The Paternal Pride of Maurice Sendak." *The New York Times*, 8 Nov. 1987.

Kumar, Mohan B., and Michael Tjepkema, "Suicide Among First Nations People, Métis and Inuit (2011–2016): Findings from the 2011 Canadian Census Health and Environment Cohort." Statistics Canada, 28 June 2019, https://www150.statcan.gc.ca/n1/pub/99-011-x/99-011-x2019001-eng.htm.

Levithan, David. *Answers in the Pages.* Penguin Random House, 2023.

Lewis, C.S. *The Lion, The Witch, and The Wardrobe.* Geoffrey Bles, 1950.

Mosionier, Beatrice. *In Search of April Raintree.* 40th anniversary ed., HighWater Press, 2023.

Robertson, David A. *All the Little Monsters: How I Learned to Live with Anxiety*. Harper Collins Canada, 2025.

Robertson, David A. *The Barren Grounds*. The Misewa Saga, Book One. Tundra Books, 2021.

Robertson, David A. *Betty: The Helen Betty Osborne Story*. Illustrated by Scott B. Henderson. HighWater Press, 2012.

Robertson, David A. *The Great Bear*. The Misewa Saga, Book Two. Tundra Books, 2022.

Robertson, David A. *Ispík kákí péyakoyak/When We Were Alone*. Illustrated by Julie Flett, translated by Alderick Leask. Bilingual ed., Swampy Cree/English Edition. HighWater Press, 2020.

Robertson, David A. *7 Generations: A Plains Cree Saga*. Illustrated by Scott B. Henderson. Compiled ed., HighWater Press, 2012.

Robertson, David A. *Sugar Falls: A Residential School Story*. Illustrated by Scott B. Henderson. HighWater Press, 2011.

Robertson, Donald. "Speaking in Tongues." Unpublished manuscript, 1993.

Robinson, Paul, Taylor Small, Anna Chen, and Mark Irving. "Over-Representation of Indigenous Persons in Adult Provisional Custody, 2019/2020 and 2020/2021." Statistics Canada, 12 July 2023, https://www150.statcan.gc.ca/n1/pub/85-002-x/2023001/article/00004-eng.htm.

Wagner, Erica. "'Writing Is Always an Act of Hope': Margaret Atwood on *The Testaments*." *The New Statesman*, 18 Sept. 2019, https://www.newstatesman.com/culture/2019/09/writing-is-always-an-act-of-hope-margaret-atwood-on-the-testaments.

CLC Kreisel Lecture Series

Published by University of Alberta Press and the Centre for
Literatures in Canada / Centre de littératures au Canada

Un art de vivre par temps de catastrophe
DANY LAFERRIÈRE
ISBN 978-0-88864-553-1

The Sasquatch at Home
Traditional Protocols & Modern Storytelling
EDEN ROBINSON
ISBN 978-0-88864-559-3

Imagining Ancient Women
ANNABEL LYON
ISBN 978-0-88864-629-3

Dear Sir, I Intend to Burn Your Book
An Anatomy of a Book Burning
LAWRENCE HILL
ISBN 978-0-88864-679-8

Dreaming of Elsewhere
Observations on Home
ESI EDUGYAN
ISBN 978-0-88864-821-1

A Tale of Monstrous Extravagance
Imagining Multilingualism
TOMSON HIGHWAY
ISBN 978-1-77212-041-7

Who Needs Books?
Reading in the Digital Age
LYNN COADY
ISBN 978-1-77212-124-7

The Burgess Shale
The Canadian Writing Landscape of the 1960s
MARGARET ATWOOD
ISBN 978-1-77212-301-2

Wisdom in Nonsense
Invaluable Lessons from My Father
HEATHER O'NEILL
ISBN 978-1-77212-377-7

Most of What Follows Is True
Places Imagined and Real
MICHAEL CRUMMEY
ISBN 978-1-77212-457-6

An Autobiography of the Autobiography of Reading
DIONNE BRAND
ISBN 978-1-77212-508-5

A Short History of the Blockade
Giant Beavers, Diplomacy and Regeneration in Nishnaabewin
LEANNE BETASAMOSAKE SIMPSON
ISBN 978-1-77212-538-2

Next Time There's a Pandemic
VIVEK SHRAYA
ISBN 978-1-77212-605-1

An Anthology of Monsters
How Story Saves Us from Our Anxiety
CHERIE DIMALINE
ISBN 978-1-77212-682-2

Toward an Anti-Racist Poetics
WAYDE COMPTON
ISBN 978-1-77212-743-0

Bodies of Art, Bodies of Labour
KATE BEATON
ISBN 978-1-77212-800-0

Every Story Is a Call to Action
DAVID A. ROBERTSON
ISBN 978-1-77212-851-2

20th Anniversary Kreisel Lecture
LISE GABOURY-DIALLO, SHANI MOOTOO, and RICHARD VAN CAMP
March 2026